YEAR OF REVERSIBLE LOSS

Norma Farber

EL LEÓN LITERARY ARTS/ANDREA YOUNG ARTS
A DEUX FRÈRES BOOK

Year of Reversible Loss is published by
El León Literary Arts/Andrea Young Arts
A Deux Frères Book

Publisher: Thomas Farber
Managing Editor: Kit Duane
Cover and Book Design: Andrea Young

For sales information contact:
Small Press Distribution, Inc.
1341 Seventh Street
Berkeley, CA 94710
www.spdbooks.org

www.elleonliteraryarts.org
www.andreayoungarts.com

ISBN 978-0-9833919-4-4
LIBRARY OF CONGRESS CATALOG NUMBER: 2011940995
PRINTED IN USA

ACKNOWLEDGEMENTS

Accent
Arion's Dolphin
Christian Century
Blue Unicorn
Boston Monthly
Christian Science Monitor
Counter/Measure
Harvard Magazine
Harvard Medical Alumni Bulletin
Horn Book Magazine
New Yorker
New York Times
Poetry Northwest
Quarterly Review of Literature
Radcliffe Quarterly
Snowy Egret
Spirit
Voices
Wind
Yankee

for myself and strangers
—Gertrude Stein

CONTENTS

I. April: *Like a bright exhalation in the evening*

II. May: *Strongly spent is synonymous with kept*

III. June: *If music be the food*

IV. July: *How do you recognize losses?*

V. August: *Teach, delight, and move*

VI. September: *I had not thought death had undone so many*

VII. October: *A journey is forever lonely and parallel to death*

VIII. November: *LET: v. transitive: to permit, allow, suffer*

IX. December: *But. But is a place where they can cease to distress her*

X. January: *So here it is at last, the distinguished thing*

XI. February: *Not choose not to be*

XII. March: *What thou lovest well, shall not be reft from thee*

*The single poetic theme of Life and Death. . .
the question of what survives of the beloved.*

—Alun Lewis

Like a bright exhalation in the evening
—Shakespeare, *Henry VIII*

Last night you died.

You phoned always at the end of your workday. "I'm leaving now, *Lieb*. Anything you'd like me to bring?"

"No, nothing, *Lieb*."

The usual exchange.

I put the roast in the oven. By the time it is done, and well done, you have been discovered unconscious at your desk. By the time I have told those who should be told, you are no longer ill.

> Sign your name on the wind.
> Then I'll know which way
> to follow you.

> How silent my body feels:
> hush of my shoulders
> upholding the weightlessness of loss.

> A gaunt moon.
> I need more light
> to free the stone from its shadow.

For the good of the trees, the gardener has pruned the dogwood in the plantings fifteen storeys below. He has given me this six-foot branch to force into bloom.

> Pursed winter-tight,
> the dead-brown lip-bracts clench fast.
> Will hidden tongues never sing?

> Strange genesis,
> the morning after death
> resembles older siblings.

Between the river and the road:

> Now that I gaze deeper:
> the joggers run steadier,
> the traffic races faster,
> the water flows surer.

> Dry diamond dust:
> the river sparkles again
> in the flooding sun.

> *The dew, the dew!*
> No sooner said
> than gone.

Of the sycamore:

> Old shag-bark giant ball-swinger,
> even yet in April
> playing the dangled felt of your bells.

> Skeins of raveled willow branches,
> this yellowing early April.
> Thought is a tangled yarn.

Why mention spring
mixing memory and desire?
Words barely outlive the season.

Of the hyacinth:

From the shadow-belled pagoda
a clanging toll
of dusk-blue tower.

Of the dogwood:

Some humorous finger
tickles the crease of the bud,
teases the folds
into twin shingles overlapping.

Of the recurring sun:

At high noon
neither the derelict nor the diplomat
casts a shadow.

Though I lean to the west
in the late afternoon,
the head of my shadow inclines east.

Night has a giant thirst,
draining sun to the dregs.
Are there yet more casks?

I rise before the sun,
to see the sun rise.
I say *Sunrise!*—and it's happened.

Of the alder:

> After so hard long spasm of catkin cluster,
> of winter frozen purple with endurance:
> look, overnight, a ruddy loosening.

Of the dogwood:

> Dead-brown, the outer bracts.
> But tenderer, inner under-lips
> press between the plastron margins,
> flouting the cold.

What is this civil need to tame the act of April? I bring a branch indoors to raise it in a room. Domesticate the bud? Rescue it from the wild? I call my neighbors in to see me let my dogwood grow. My bough! *my* bloom!—now that I give it vase and water.

> In what sense are you mine, love,
> since nothing in my possession
> can detain you?
>
> I shoot these words
> as arrows toward you.
> Let me hear the rip of target.
>
> It is serious enough
> that sun is not sun for you.
> But that darkness, even...
>
> Closets cleared,
> drawers emptied of haberdashery.
> Every millimeter crowded with reminiscence.

Not to see the horizon
for the fog,
can be called a relief.

Of the dogwood:

A sudden dozen tongues
push the light-green cheeks apart.
I lean to hear the cheep of silence.

That dirt-brown, stone-brown hibernator bud turns overnight to chalice. A sacral tinge stains all the linings of a four-scaled cup.

Let this container keep,
so I may drink its look
of silken chrysolite.

The blossom ripens. Each bract a map of longitudes, each carries a burnished scar: brownish, dryish, hardish edge, memento of the bud. O immemorial cicatrice!

Let me not now or ever
defect from watching rapt
my transient world.

Of maple keys:

A dozen cloven wands
pelting my head:
green-bottle bruise.

Farther and farther the dogwood bracts bend back, dancers arching away from horizontal. They curve and curl and lean at length: after much early haste and vigor, arrived—it appears—at a destination. They wait, plant-patient, stretched serenely, serenely twisting, no single form the duplicate of another. Their edges lift like arms, or shoulders shrugged. Each bract's a little chute, a pitcher mouth. Their fine intoxication flows that slippery course. Wholesome pallor seeps throughout the four-fold recumbency. Presto! and every bract's for its own self. This wide one swells still wider, whirling away from symmetry, closing its gulley to make the sluice of light slow down. Dippers and ladles, gutters and culverts, no two alike, they scoop their scarves, they toss their banners, unfold their moth-wings, preen their hundred images.

Of the course of dogwood:

> At a certain split second
> green is white.
> Uncertain: when.

> Freedom of the bract,
> pinned at the base,
> to fly its full length and breadth.

> Secret in the bud:
> the hidden fury to be single, self,
> beyond resemblance.

> Through the mesh of city noises,
> the single crow-throat:
> *I caw, I am!*

Today I watch the terminal spectacle. Nothing further than this, this farthest stretch of bract, the round green inflorescences elongated, gold-dusted with pollen-waving stamens, climax of the house-blooming branch.

> For this, the pruning cut.
> For this, the care.
> For this, the watch, the waiting.
> For this extreme arrival.

How much longer to applaud the singed, aging life? How much to ask of life, that it live and live in forms coincident with my delight?

> In the vast planting under sky,
> whether I watch or not,
> things bloom and die, or not.

How restricted my interest, compared to nature's, that can contain both birth and death, dying and undying, pleat folding and wrinkle shriveling, with equal countenance, with no sign of disparagement. To welcome grey revealed with green, the hem-stitched leaf with the unperverted, the mined vein beside the original, the fine bobbin foliage-ruin natural as hunger, gall of the oak—God's young wasp.

For nature, everything is taking place in a first place. A beginning. Beginning bud, beginning seed, beginning dissolution. Let me explore that furthest incipience. *Handsels of our joys hereafter?*

> Always beginning,
> love is always.
> *So be beginning.*

> Who needs a phoenix?
> In the right season of listening
> a robin sings so roundly.

Strongly spent is synonymous with kept
—Robert Frost

Now the dogwood outdoors is in full bloom. Layers of cruciform snowflakes suspended in the lower air: a frosty contradiction of the surrounding season. A fountain May-frozen.

This gush and growth strangely invade me. Personal loss has warned me to guard my response, economize my joy. It has behooved me to observe a frugal, flinty resistance.

But nature proves indifferent, whether to my reluctance or my rapture. Trees are plumping and polishing, filing their buds with the wind of the same welcome. Why should I think it would be otherwise? Or that I'd not be fingering the glue of the horsechestnut with a child's delight—to be sticky myself with what will be green—*green, green, green,* even without you?

> A diamond-cutter's at work,
> splitting the glaze of the bud,
> faceting the leaf.
>
> Proof of the past:
> what never was acquired
> cannot be spent.

Loss. Just to pronounce *loss,* to lift my tongue and lay it down, is a kind of sigh. The meaning of loss is what haunts these wealthy May phenomena. Loss of focus? For I can't find you there at the center, or precisely anywhere. Not bound, are you, all parts of

you, into the old purpose, the plan? Not winding the clock, set-
ting the alarm? Not starting awake at the jangle, not leaping to the
day's demand? Enfranchised, yes. Dispersing wider than any one
life allows. Dissipating finely into the thousands, ten thousands.

> How to recollect
> a disseminated dust
> into one man, detained?

Of the sycamore:

> Hard as the hard green ball,
> to believe the unyielding sphere
> will soften to fluff.

Of the redbud:

> Blood from a stone,
> a rich red life oozing
> out of the very rock-bole.

I'm losing the pinpoint of you. Fullness, manifold, overwhelms
me. Not one but a dozen limbs of the black willow diverge from
the trunk, splintering the wind in a spidery fireworks. Name me
the single branch, the long true wand among many. Find me
the twig, the one and only. Pollard the stump and presto! the
pate's grown antlers, dense, divided, spreading a low green hair-
split coif. The *you*, the *you*! The crown's so numberous—where
to invent some principal part? The clue's escaped in an overall
sea. Cables and layers of leafage. Impossible to fix on a simple
emblem. Seized by multiples, outnumbered, overpowered. I reel
from richness.

> Even the stone I stand on
> teeters in lichen,
> totters in shadow.

The weight of love:
measurable
as the ponder of light.

Granted, shadows never broke a rock.
Yet look at them,
how they bring it to tremble!

I lean to the podocarpus to learn co-existence. I pause to check
the green chinks for late news of limpet aphid or white lint of
mealybug. A leaf puckered since last night? The limbs a little bald-
er than last week? There are ways which move counter to my guess
and preference.

Nonetheless, praise
is in the eye of the beholder.
Praise can even look askance.

A honeybee has flown all the way up to my fifteenth floor. One
would like to thank him for the favor.

Industrious hope,
how many cells
in your sharpsweet hive?

I rise early to catch the sun arriving. I'm running out of meta-
phors: I've seen it happen so often. Reprise, reprise! Truly, there
are no new images. Doesn't the sun resort, forever, to reconnoi-
tered skies? Doesn't it crack the same morning pistol?

Of the dandelion:

All yolk
this poach of sun
on stem.

MAY

Of the crab-trees:

> Cameo-pink parachutes on my Cambridge shore.
> On yours, that other, what's blooming?
> Or is this the one-strand river?

> Sun-fire in the river!
> Don't try to douse it,
> it won't burn.

> Magical welts on the river-skin.
> Someone, something under the fine contusions.
> A point, an Excalibur.

> My arms the holding shores,
> could I but keep you
> a known flow, going.

Of shadows:

> Great oaks casting great dark pools.
> My need is small
> as the dusk under a lilac bush.

> Under the hero,
> under the deserter,
> the shadow's one and the same color.

There's no way of hoarding these copious hours. Impossible to space out the abundance of bloom, to tide me through the year. This is the very month of flowering trees, greening trees, coppering trees. This is earth as given, the only one I know given.

Of the buttercup:

> With a live stem for axle,
> the wheel of shellac'd petals
> transports me at small risk.

You must have approved, in your time, of May-month particularly: of the strong showering of gifts, so like your own abundance and spending. Somewhere there might be a planet on which parsimony or moderation is the guiding principle, Not here. You and the earth: so alike. For you both, *to be* signifying *to give*. A wasteful wealth? A prodigal bestowing? Neither of you was ever the poorer for the spending. And the rest of us so much the richer.

Your mother told a story of you in your childhood. You were perhaps eight years old, she recalled, when you were rewarded, one Saturday, for having cleaned and polished her coal-burning stove. In those days, in that place, a nickel bought a large bag of candy. You held out the bag for your siblings—half a dozen or so by then—to reach into. When they had all taken a share, the bag held nothing for you but a few small chips. Memoir has it that you fisted the bag into a tight ball, and hurled it at the stove! Your sense of justice properly outraged. But later, when it was yourself you gave, out of that deep cornucopia of your own person, the supply proved bottomless. The pitcher of Philemon and Baucis. To think I tasted of that source. And still taste.

> It can't harm to hope
> your dust enjoys this May noon,
> your lustrous particles bathing in sunfall.

In this first year of loss, I search everywhere for proof of its denial. The poet writes: "Strongly spent is synonymous with kept." You spent strongly; you are lost to me; therefore I keep you. Thus, skeletally—yet a breathing armature—runs my brief. What, exactly, do I keep?

MAY

Very few mementos.

A gold-headed cane, respectfully inscribed.

A large cross-bow and the diploma certifying you duly installed
as a member of the Guild of St. George of Ghent.

> *Wij, Deken, Koning, Proviseerders en verdere*
> *Leden van het Souverein Gilde van den Edelen*
> *Ridder St.-Joris, onderhouden met den kruisboog,*
> *binnen de Stad Gent, verklaren dat de Heer Dr.*
> *Sidney Farber van Boston (Mass.) U.S.A. is*
> *aangenomen als Confreer, van ons Gilde en dat*
> *hij als dusdanig moet worden erkend door aile*
> *Gilden, waar hij zich zal anbieden.*

A small ivory-inlaid cross-bow, an award from your medical col-
leagues. It bears the inscription: *A little child shall lead them.*

A child, children, led you. The child that is a man, a woman. I
remember a Sunday morning, nearly fifty years ago. We were in
your laboratory at the Hospital. An autopsy permission had just
been granted. You invited me to watch. I stayed briefly, then sat
in an adjoining room. An unforgettably beautiful child, in her
helplessness. And you, radiantly alive as you traced the secret
inroads of death. You making the first neat incision. You in the
precise presence of death. You wresting a hidden life-hope from
death. The image of the two of you: life and death in closest
involvement. Life learning from death. And death yielding its
life-giving disclosures. "Life is why I was drawn to pathology, the
study of disease," you said.

I'm drawn to examine *loss.* In order to define *keeping.*

> The black blackbird:
> shadow of the white blackbird,
> so rare it's never seen.

MAY

The black hole gapes
where a galaxy slips so far
it sinks into its opposite.

Not to look back in love,
not to bereave us doubly.
To keep you unseen at my back.

To keep fired by you,
a copper beech burning
without consuming.

JUNE

If music be the food
—Shakespeare, *Twelfth Night*

Memorials can be absurd. Last week I watched the vivid bands of boys and girls, men and women, on their way to the cemetery. From my fifteenth storey, they looked like brightly garbed marionette regiments and daughters-of-regiments, out of some light-opera central European principality. The army jeeps following them were tiny playthings. If the figures had simply paraded, silently, I might have watched with a little amusement, wistfully. But each battalion blared out its own memorial utterance as it moved: a march, a hymn, a drum-roll, a rock-tune. Their endeavors overlapped, so that there were periods when the varieties had to be listened to together. The counterpoint was not convincing. On such occasions, freedom of choice among the members can disrupt the intended effect of the ensemble. Ceremony requires a strong guiding management.

On celebrating a loss:

> Speak up, loss! You subside
> soft as laburnum cascading.
> I need to hear the petals fall.

How much of nature happens in silence! The unfolding of fern from snail to fringe. The deepening of dye in the June green. Wisteria draining from purple to lavender. There may be music too high for our hardness of hearing. Every act, every change, however gradual, may vibrate with its altered condition. Music may be more pervasive than ever guessed.

Those rain-opals on the rose,
what a hush of clatter
when sun scoops them up.

Half-syllable, half-caesura, a mystery twitches the mouth of leaf,
wing, whitecap with so low a verb interfacing the silences, we
have to cup our need to catch the hiss.

Heard early and June-ascendent:
a note that keeps the pitch
of clematis-blue.

Fee-bee! sings a phoebe.
Tree-tulips open their throat:
Liriodendron tulipifera!

Music must have been the first food, the first breaking of
bread. I shared it with my mother: music of the blood river-
ing through me, from her, and back to her. Pouring from her
mountain sources, returning to her largeness, in the way of va-
pors and clouds. Sheltered as I lay in that early enclosure, I had
no need to hear grosser sounds of the outside world. I could
curl into her, into myself, and listen with my inner attention
to pulses and portamentoes so fine of intonation, I never later
could retrieve them, never, afterward, refer to them with assur-
ance. Only sometimes, in the less-than-stillness of a zephyr, in
the more-than-stillness of an embrace, I could almost recapture
an old knowledge: This song I have heard before. Clearer than
now, or ever after.

For the clamoring orchestras of the world flung themselves
against my ears, even before my own first noisy debut. I was a
drum, roundly slapped. I laughed till I cried. The attendant
drummer laughed. My listeners laughed and applauded. I heard
voices and instruments in chorus and singly: recitatives of ex-
clamations, florid sighs, plangent cooings, clucks and staccatos.
And bravura arias—surely—of adoration. For every birth contains

that time of a carol in the straw:

> Hey diddle manger,
> o welcome the stranger,
> the kings have been handed cigars.
> The little boy laughs to burst the bin,
> and the hole in the roof's full of stars.

O I knew the feelings, the tremblings and emotions, of my world by their sheer elemental sounds. But their nuances of meaning escaped me. I was too fresh in this place. The scale of its diction rang foreign. The winds that blew about me had as yet no grammar. I could discern only that they were blowing. They were a music, moving.

> (In the house where I was born,
> even the plumbing
> sang a tune.)

When in time, and increasingly, I detected words in the wind, it was as though I now knew where the winds were coming from, where they were going. And this news seemed good to know, and to account for. The winds brought me a message as well as a music: an intimation, or even an explicit meaning. Sometimes quite simple and mundane. "A north wind is blowing, put on your sweater, darling." Or strange yet familiar, an ancient tiding: "Rockabye baby, on the tree-top." I understood, and I didn't. I seized the innocent tune, and never tired of it. It was always newly haunting, aching and sweet, comforting and disturbing.

> Let me sing out
> the world's question.
> I want to be answerable.

In my need I began to note the text; in a beginner's way, to approach it. "Down will come cradle, baby and all." Yes, I could perceive it, hear it, understand it, almost feel it—the hazard of it, the huge cataclysm it predicted. Yet simultaneously the tune's reassuring cadence, the tender yet firm conclusion on the tonic, rescued from imminent peril. Music gentled the fall. I lay protected in an embrace which reconciled danger with delight.

> To make songs of loss,
> and lose it,
> keeping only the music.
>
> The longest day.
> Never long enough
> to perpetuate the cadence.
>
> Someone I knew
> now knows the noise
> of nothing.
>
> The robin after rain
> gurgles momentously:
> white water in a stony brook.

Thus I learned that the meanings of the world were meaningless without the world's music at the same instant at once delineating and diddling, defining and defying them—even denying them. A marvelous counterpoint beyond counterpoint. Not only the notes of the scale were in it, their values and intervals, but vowels, consonants, syllables, rhymes. My apprehension of *music* expanded till it encompassed worlds upon worlds of dynamics and diversities. Words were contained in it, or it was embraced in words—I could no longer make the distinction. All I dared know was that a certain utterable experience constituted my breathing, my very surviving. Sometimes shallow, as in sleep. Sometimes rapid as in flight or intense emotion. Sometimes especially steady and deep, as when I was construing a fresh music of my own, which I called, indiscriminately, *song* or *poem*.

Sing me the bobbin-leaf spinning.
Say me the spun city-dust.
There is yet hope in ailanthus.

Amplitude of the catalpa,
secreting nectar
even at the base of the leaf!

Of night-music:

No second disc to meet it,
how can one moon, one cymbal, play?
Listen, with your eyes.

If the bread I broke with the world was music, the cup I
shared was words.

To fall awake,
consecutive mornings,
by choice, *by choice*!

Falling, to grab at a hair.
If it's not there?
Grabbing may thread the air.

Nearly July. I know,
by the way aromas of basswood
lope across the street.

Riddled with insect-holes,
the askew leaf-hearts of linden
gape with light.

Your words and music: all this while I seek to define the
words and music of you. I am thinking, for instance, of a
flower called goldthread.

JUNE

As if you were a bell to be struck,
or a bird to be listened to,
still I search for the sound of you,
the note that names you.

And it happens that surprising utterance
waits hidden
as a root of wildflower
under moistened woods.

Crowfoot leaves shine wide evergreen
beneath showy white sepals.
Uncertain, I pull at the stem.
An underground string comes up, blood-gold.

Light plucks the length, and it sings.

How do you recognize losses?
—Gertrude Stein

Knowing that I shall lose it
over and over and over
I accept the universe.

Now that the longest day lies a fortnight past, I can hope soon to waken early enough to catch the sunrise again.

Why is it a failed, a lost day if I miss the start of it?

With stronger suns of spring, that crack of light shatters earlier and earlier. March dawns were still reasonable. I could be there, taking due notice as light spread late, after the long dark. Aggressive spring brilliance enforces its demand of attendance. Winter was a less insistent host.

April, May, June.

Stricter demand, more and more to lose, that I shouldn't be losing. I pay high rent for the view, raised over the river and clear to the eastern skyline. Costly to oversleep.

To be in at the beginning is a way of upholding whatever the hours bring: a responsible witness, as though I stood at the world's creation, nodding *It's good.*

That it needs to be good, is the deepest thing I know.

Beginnings are fluent, a down-current ride to the sea. My craft is light, fitted to the river as a kiss to lips. I am lean, laughing, ready for voyage. The wind makes spider's webs of the water. Then a breeze unwinds them. I bruise the surface—the ripples complain but slightly. This early current's *with* me, not minding supporting me. Plenty of gallons beneath me. I won't go aground.

> A certain hunger
> wants to be kept
> going to sea.

O I'll go far this morning, till the sun that rises arrests my shadow. Alone, without that thinnest company, I'll hit the tide at noon. Then shadows change.

Whatever reverses I suffer at sea, I'll keep as a spar this run of the river that starts at dawn. Capsized, I can hang onto it. It may even float me to shore. It's my hope, my buoyant holding.

For I was there when night had submerged the sun—as though beyond revival. But I was there and held a hand to morning, barely bobbed up, faint yet breathing, gasping for very bleeding life. I reached toward morning and it was preserved. It might have drowned, otherwise. In a late hour I'll remember assisting at sunrise.

> In a hard hour
> memory pays out
> the lifeline.

Remembrance of the dead can joyously salvage the living. Where Peter Stuyvesant and hundreds of his descendants and other historic folk are buried, a playground takes form. Bricks and cobblestones are laid in arching and circular designs, around dozens of flat gravestones. Here at St. Mark's Church-in-the-Bowery, the way to honor the dead is not to die with them but to live. *To try to live.*

That woman of Masada, trying to live...

This crew of diggers, nearly two thousand years after: unearth-
ing Herodian magnificence, frescoes and mosaics, silence of
pillared drums, unsupporting bases, unsupported Corinthian
capitals. Fragments of platters, the walls and the entries, and the
vacant bench, the unpeopled stairway.

All these have been uncovered. It is enough.

> Twenty thousand waves of day
> have come over me.
> Still not enough for drowning.

Furthermore the earlier staircase, the Ionic capitals. And the
intimate bath-houses, no steam issuing. Enough.

Water cisterns, clay pipes, and the oven beyond, the hot-room
itself, hardly an opening in it. The niche where the huge quartz
tub was standing: a mine to match Pompeii, Herculaneum.
Enough, enough!

> May was more than enough.
> June was my surfeit.
> Let me give back July.

And the gathering up of the particled vessel...

> Such promise as a stone holds:
> this hard oblong
> under the green peachdown.

Moreover the cold-room, the tepid-room, the disrobing-room, the
floor paved with tiles of black and white. Dolomite slabs of the
double-rowed walls of storehouses. Pierced moulds, restorable
jars, for oil, for wine, for flour, each in its keeping-place. And
flasks. And juglets. Enough of recollection.

> The airing of the gulls delights me.
> If I'm bereaved,
>   it's no concern of theirs.

The administration center, the shrewd gate where a single watchman could guard the whole compound. Enough of resurrection!

Casemate 1,039, the creased raglet of scroll, psalming *honey out of the rock.*

If they had found merely coins, but not the cosmetics...*Enough!*

If merely arrows, but not the jettisoned mirror-case...*Enough!*

Fibulae, but not buckles.

Ring keys, but not signet rings.

Oil-lamps, but not the used faggots.

The gold breast-plate, but not, not the charred bones...*It would have been enough!*

All the sorer then, in the amiable tabernacle, to grapple the gnawed parchment, thin as newspaper, beholding the vision of Ezekiel.

This expedition is set down on a mountain full of disordered bones. And lo, they are very dry.

Dry as centuries on the tongue, the summons of the last lottery. Desert air parches the shards. Those last eleven still live, their nickname plain on the ostraca. Whose lot to kill, whose to be killed?

Come from the four winds, o breath, and breathe upon these slain...an exceeding great army.

If the leaving could be easy,
as a child leaves its shadow
at the end of the swing's arc…

That woman of Masada, leaving.

Laden with loot of the sea,
we are leaving behind us the heaviest shells
and the longest things of weed…

That woman of Masada, leaving the dead.

Selecting a residue jettison,
keeping the prime,
the pick of the combing.

That woman of Masada, leaving the dead, trying to live.

Later we chuck in the discard
an image, another, another, retaining but two,
then one, none, not even a starfish, not even a…

Take me to that cave, that close escape, that fearsome ground where crouched the woman Josephus called superior to most in prudence and learning.

Leave the late fortress where zealots in hundreds died by violent self-design: families at the faltering hands of fathers; fathers by lot at the cut of the last destroyer, himself despatched by his own thrust, in the throes of his fallen kin.

Take me to her, abiding, who hid in a cave and in consequence rescued (it must be) her children and the old grandmother—from both swords: of her own tribe, of the triumphing enemy.

Could there be loss
rubbed so smooth
the sun lusters it?

Quiet,
cruciform,
mustard memorializes its gold.

Brash St. Johnswort
takes its strident yellow
from the risen sun.

A warm wind from the south
lifts the ash-tree foliage palmside up.
Every silver hand says, Come!

Overtake me with dissent as a widow who dares be discovered
infamous in survival. O how dared she lessen the forfeit, the
grandeur of that consummate kill? How dared she extenuate
death? How dare I confront her as she emerges, straightening,
proud, purposeful, support of her mother-in-law (it must be); an
infant on her shoulder, the others clenched at her skirt.

She girds her losses, outliving a thousand martyrs.

Can there be loss
worn so thin
the sun shines through?

Sun-struck,
the sycamore strips its rags,
revealing an orient flesh.

Praise the weed purslane
for spurring new plants
from torn bits of stem.

Under numberless trees and innumerable leaves:
uncountable grass.
I look because I look because I look...

Teach, delight, and move
—Franciscus Junius

HEART (680 grams):
    RIGHT ATRIUM – DILATATION AND HYPERTROPHY, MODERATE
    RIGHT VENTRICLE –
        HYPERTROPHY (0.3 -0.5 cm.)
        DILATATION, MODERATE
        FOCAL FIBROSIS
    LEFT ATRIUM – DILATATION AND HYPERTROPHY, MODERATE
    LEFT VENTRICLE –
        HYPERTROPHY (1.5 cm.) and DILATATION
        OLD HEALED INFARCTIONS, ANTERO-SEPTAL
        AND POSTEROLATERAL (5 x 4 cm. and
        9 x 7 cm. RESPECTIVELY)
    POSTERIOR WALL –
        THINNING TO 0.4 cm., WITH FIBROUS
        SCARRING OF WALL.

I am drawn, once again, to Rembrandt's *Anatomy of Dr. Tulp.*

Rembrandt visited the public anatomies of Leiden and Amsterdam. Like his pictorial record of them, they were designed to instruct, to entertain, to move.

    Chicory blue,
    that blue the sky reflects
    between cloudgusts of clover.

The pathologist has sent me this autopsy report. Your terminal episode was probably an arrhythmia, or a very recent extension of your infarction.

Of the larch:

> Tree decidedly to my taste:
> deciduous,
> with the look of everlast.

Whatever you were, you are no longer. This is the message of the funerary theater. A life has withered. The innermost secrets are brought to light. Heart, lungs, liver, spleen, stomach, kidneys, all parts yield their lesson to the living. How astonishing *in situ,* the human accidents. In the remains of the defunct we learn the varieties of our enemy death. And since the bodies on anatomical display in those Renaissance theaters were the *corpora vilia* of criminals, the answers were found, by paradox, in the most degrading specimens. Evil-doers did well in dying. Skins without voices, they told truths.

> Dawn of the dandelion moons,
> morning of silent planets
> swum, full rounds, to foamy view.

Questions from the audience are admissible, provided they are decent and serious.

Let me ask, then, with Petrarch: In human affairs, what thing is greater than Death?

Our ancestors have recognized that magnitude. They make the grandest spectacle of public anatomies. "Furthermore a properly adapted theater should be located in a spacious and well-ventilated place, with ranks of seats like those of an amphitheater... The seating arrangement is to be according to rank."

> Royal, at the river's edge,
> a stately solitary pair
> of loosestrife.

> Inflated head
> of the bladder campion.
> Often crowned.

How proudly the living cling to their substance. Nor will they permit one of their favored kind to be counted among the anatomized cadavers. Only the half-lives, the criminal and the unfit, may be ritualized in this high-ranking entertainment. "Only humble and unknown persons, then, and those from distant regions may rightly be claimed for dissection, that there shall be no outrage to neighbors or relatives. Those are chosen who have been strangled by hanging and who are middle-aged, neither lean nor fat, and of rather large frame, that their components may be of more generous size and more distinctly visible to the onlookers."

> This golden girth of day
> is shriveling in its skin.
> The sack is leaking its summer light.

How every disguise, every distancing of death, reveals its wry failure. The secrets of nature we are probing on the autopsy table— these are our very own consuming mysteries.

> A first leaf shivers out of the air.
> Now let the mind begin to shed
> what shudders in the cold.

Of the new moon:

> Can't see the bird,
> only the platinum talon.
> Can't guess the bough it's gripping.

We can't forego pomp and drama. Death continues to be cause for display, for celebration. Our practice of funeral rites continues, a parallel to Rembrandt's spectacle of the dissection-table. Both stimulate excitement. The post-mortem examination has long since been removed from the arena of public entertainment. But funeral ceremonies persist, prepared exercises in morality and metaphysics. Also, perhaps, in aesthetics. And in self-defense?

> Sensitive shoot honed into armor:
> the leaf of the thistle
> is consumed by few creatures.

If I can discover a moral or a metaphysic in death, maybe I shall be finding a means to rationalize loss. Yet I must admit that the longer and closer I live with loss, the less it allows itself to be "interpreted", manipulated. Death exists. Loss *is*.

> Whoso loses the life of another—
> what does he find
> save its loss?

We spend too many centuries of our histories, decades of our lives, converting, controverting (subverting?) a simple fact. Shouldn't we rather support our observation with sensitive recognition? To live *sub specie mortis*: is it more threatening than to live under the sun, our life-giver? Isn't it of the same order?

> The end is the end
> only while I wait
> uncertainly for it.

> From green to taupe,
> the fruit of my fig-tree ripens
> till I consume it.

From green to deep, we ripen into the mouth of death. What shade are you now?

> No wind, a dead-still space.
> Sails hang, clouds pall.
> A stasis of staying.

> Even harder than proceeding:
> delaying.
> As for tinder to dry.

> Color starts to flake.
> Metallic ragweed sculpture
> rusts along the river.

But we are moving, moving...In reality there's no such state as arrest. Inventing a halt, we take pictures of ourselves, of one another. Portraiture as an art form has been closely linked with death. The loss of individual personality may be counter-measured by a realistic painting. We record our perishable appearances as a hopeful safeguard against that certain something further. Louis, Duc d'Orléans is saluted for his ordinance (1403): "que la remembrance de mon visage et de mes mains soit faicte sur ma tombe en guise de mort."

> How shall I know danger?
> The dove can look a hawk,
> so free it swoops.

I'm tempted to discard all your photographs. They no longer resemble you, my remembrance of you, which is changing as certainly as I change.

Of the half-moon:

> That gilded roof, high, humped,
> just fits the night
> as a dome its building.

> Both are tilting.

Of the locust pod:

> A single season's tannery
> will turn this suede green pelt
> to tough brown hide.

I keep at hand a snapshot of you and an infant grandson. You are seated, holding him in your lap. He holds your thumb. You stare gently yet fixedly at each other: his look as serious as yours. A search flows both ways between you, each of you seeking some answer, some certification from the other. You are both in profile: the lines of half your forehead, the heavy lid of an eye, your flat left cheek and intricacies of ear; Billy's sweet arc of brow and solemn upward gray-blue glance, his round cheek, his definitive—already!—intricacies of ear. On the diaper under his head an eighth-inch shadow silhouettes his features. From a vase behind his head a marguerite halos him modestly. Parts of fifty books are visible in the background shelves. I am making some effort to record these details. But what I really perceive, what remains with me between the occasions of looking, is the interchange between man and child, the movment, the music, back and forth, like no song ever heard sung. Music, as we are accustomed to experience it, advances in time. This song between you and Billy advances and reverses. No, it moves instantaneously in both directions. It's a moving suspension, a two-way flow. The flow is what I'm after. A current between us. Is it possible?

Now let us celebrate division,
for love arises between,
only between.

A hint, an intimation only? Like those flashes of carp I almost
saw in the June river?

"Knowledge is memory."
Then it is ignorance I pursue,
a forgotten future.

Of the resinous tree of memory:

Keep flowing,
never fixing time
into stone timelessness.

Today, walking again by the river, I saw plainly a flat dead
orange ellipse floating on the surface. No need to guess at it, the
corpse was there, an object, definitive, static. The interchange
was missing, the interplay between fish and flood. My search con-
tinues, like yours and Billy's. The search continues between us.

Of the full moon:

A tight drum-head,
cloud-colored as a timbal skin.
Knock, to know if music's within.

One brazen wheel
on a macadam sky.
Suppose the whole chariot.

Already a first aster
starring the weed-deep riverbank:
a reversal, sky at my feet.

I had not thought death had undone so many
—Dante

So many words about one death.

Then what can be said for the millions?

Thickets of riverbank weeds
mowed loud out of mystery.
Psst, the roots are conspiring.

An intimate spider
insinuates her thread.
The stubble's no longer discreet.

A strange, subtle increase: totality, generality of losses infiltrates my private mourning. Am I already losing you still further in a more diffuse awareness? A disturbing possibility. I have been entertaining my comfortable bereavement: a suspect comfort, focusing upon my single grief, neatly defined. The relief of precisely identified pain: toothache, earache. Whereas the ailment may be more widespread, less remediable.

The last summer moon, fainting.
Before it extinguishes,
it will spark a first frost.

Remediable? No. The analogy falters. Pain is not the equivalent of loss. Pain is *there*, located, positively removable: by a cure, by a cancellation. Not loss. At most, loss may be replaced: as a broken watch. Substituted for.

But not this loss, your loss, the loss of you.

> Light is skewered
> on the accommodating branches.
> It's so many layers of leaves.

Of the sassafras:

> Power of pungency!
> Good grooved bark,
> wood pliable as hope.

Well then, loss may be *lulled?*

> In the cage of his wings
> the cricket rubs cold fire.
> I go to gather a kindled evensong.

Yes, that's it. The music of the world, the visions, the scents, *lull* what was lately so importunate, an aching deprivation. The night jasmine's in bloom, drenching the whole apartment—an hour after sunset—with such dense fragrance, I open all the windows. The miracle of this night-flowering! This outpouring which fills the blank of evening.

> All day my eyes are stung
> by things visible,
> all night my nostrils by aromas,
> all life my pulses by hopes.

"September 17: Mercury is near the early crescent moon this evening but it will be very difficult to see either one." The Sky Chart helps me, nonetheless, guess at the unseen. Even imagined sensations delight me.

Loss and emptiness engulfed with wonder. A desertion? Am I abandoning my grief? Am I abandoning *you*, occasion of my grief? Is your name now *grief?*

> Express regret,
> sigh for the blighted elm.
> Yet stately sophora drips with pods.

> Poignantly quickened,
> lavender-thistle-pricked.
> Just by looking.

Of the true fir:

> Thumbs up!
> A thousand foam-green fingers
> grant life to the living tree.

If ever arrow reached its target, yours did. Your life transfixed the very pupil of the bullseye. The sender, whosoever, need not lament the loss of weapon.

Is your name *arrow, weapon, instrument?*

Let me, in my need, call you *continuity.* Your death itself makes continuity all the more needed.

> Ailanthus afire with seeds:
> kindle your clusters
> to raging survival!

Instruments are short-lived contrivances. I can't call you by their name. I can't let you reach your target. It must be a further place, far as Ithaca, without finality. Your death-voyaging must be prolonged, full of incident, rich with experiences I can't yet imagine. They must parallel my own survival. I demand for you the endless joy of the search, like my own, like yours as I knew you.

Of the blackberry:

> Joy of the way-station,
> arrival at jeweled ripeness:
> to be enjoyed.

> Poignance of joy:
> picking the terse berry,
> whose bramble rasps the wrist.

How the voices intertwine: the active and the passive. Try as I will, I can't maintain you forever *doing*, the *doer*. Your very deed results in your being *done to*—in a strict sense, your own doing. Each act, each growth a self-inflicted death.

> The fall of a leaf
> is a failure of leaf, not tree.
> And the fall of a tree?

Reason dictates that we accept in its entirety the experience of alteration—what we call *living*. Death might be considered simply one of the more striking phases of that process. No more harm in it, maybe, than in hibernacular law.

> Let winter kill
> all decorous extra cells,
> keep viable the gist.

Viability is the operative word. The gist, the essence, *is* viability. Not some limited instar thereof. To recognize the *virtual* in and beyond the actual: the excelling remainder.

A hard position to maintain. I waver constantly between desires: for the substantial; for the imperishable. My days are confrontations of alternatives.

Light is upheld in the tenderness of trees.
Or tree-towers are maintained by the watchfulness of light.

Light is caught in those weirs like fish.
Or the twigs are minnows sieved up by light's own filter.

An acid sharpness of light etches limbs and crotches.
Or limb-edge, crotch-blade excavate depths in the light.

So many words for one death.

And the million deaths? the billions?

Once more I turn from private loss, and go back and back again to
the old haunt: Why *me*? Why *us*? I am Pyrrha, wondering:

Why him? Why the man Deucalian?
Him with his home-made dinghy and unmatched oars
and the painter trailing?
Him among dolphins where dry goats should graze?
And a turtle straddling the oak-limbs, washed of their nests?
Why him? Why me, wrenched from the kitchen?
"Pyrrha, get in!" A pot boils over.
"Coming!" Not even the family silver salvaged.
My feet are soaked already, anyway.

Well, why him, rowing to burst his lungs?
And all around us, all the rest swirl under,
not kept up.

Why him still pulling, me still bailing?
It's a mean rain sinks so many craft
and lets ours bob alone.
Why only *us* running aground in an empty world?

Something fishy about survival...

I go back and back again to Noah and his God, whom it repenteth "that he made man on the earth; and it grieved him at his heart. And Jehovah said, I will destroy man whom I have created from the face of the ground; both man, and beast, and creeping things, and birds of the heavens...But Noah found favor..."

Of course we're descendants, you and I, of Noah's tribe. For we have found much favor in our lives. Most certainly we are of the chosen, the elite of mankind. Or so the old story would suggest. I have to remember that it was the survivors who told the tale: the others had no chance. How might they have reported?

> Glossy black pokeberries
> lean over the river
> and see themselves lusterless.

Like a fearful emblem, a death's-head banner, signal of the destitute, the perpetually hungry, a shivering hiss and whisper: a thought, *disaster!*, crawls up the flagpole of my conscience. A snaking thought, *holocaust!* This rustling in the wind could be the anguish and suspiration of those multitudes left perishing on that ancient shore. Did the Ark, escaping, hoist such a memento-burgee? Do we carry with us always the insignia of those we have abandoned?

> Where once a leaf clung,
> the ashtree wears a scar,
> a moon halted at half.

I can't equivocate, I have to admit I consider you elect: a paragon among men, your talents deeply engaged in the service of the rest of men. (Though I try not to tell it in Gath—yet I sing it aloud in the streets of my silence.) As for myself, by virtue of what privilege have I shared your life so intimately? In the very act of embracing my bonus—I need to question it. Am I, too, some sort of quasi-paragon—a Noah's wife, to be rescued through a husband's intercession?

The old Chester Pageant anticipates my dilemma and deals with it snappishly. Noah's wife is permitted her little demurrer:

> Yea, sir, set up your sail
> And row forth with evil hail,
> For, without any fail,
> I will not out of this town.
> But I have my gossips every one,
> One foot further I will not go;
> They shall not drown, by St. John!
> If I may save their life.

Of course she does indeed go a number of feet further. She does leave her cronies behind. Nor does she express a thought for all the rest of abandoned mankind.

> Praise weedy persistence:
> hawkweed, knotweed, chicory,
> dayflower, and grasses, grasses.

I find myself considering that lost remnant. I had meant to continue speaking only of your life, your death; my life with you, my loss; the shining decades, the light still lingering beyond your setting star.

> The gull arising
> sheds her caul underwater.
> Which bird to watch?

Of three gulls flying:

> An air-drawn triangle:
> equilateral to right to isosceles,
> so fast—I can't drop a perpendicular!

My thoughts keep swerving to those who live always in darkness, never having seen you, nor glowed in your radiance.

Of the cleistogamous touch-me-not:

> These lesser jewel-blooms,
> nunnishly closed to bees:
> yet, in their season, bearing.

To those who live in blackness, senselessness, for whom day-
break signifies only prolongation of their night.

> Strange residue:
> how large a portion of survival
> remains in mourning.

The ache, the aching joy, yes, joy, this single loss, joy of defini-
tion, is tinged with shame, shame for those who have not had a
wealth to lose. Who have been granted so meager a birthright—
it most resembles a deathly exhaustion. How can I speak of
loss, who continue so rich, still, in remembrance and anticipa-
tion of remembrance? How can I grieve for your going, for you,
the most endowed of all? I must grieve for *them*, the deprived,
deserted, deepest losers, who had nothing to lose. The most
deeply lost. A stone has more of life.

> Who killed Goliath?
> I, sang the stone.
> Of five the one.

The personal cry rebukes itself. Too many phrases uttered for the
one instance. Circles of loss widen, widen, widen around me...

A journey is forever lonely and parallel to death
—Eudora Welty

At home, baking bread.

This time of year induces and reinforces domesticity. For children and job-holders, vacations are a month-old memory. A bus collects young scholars on the corner deep below my window. Commuter car-traffic draws swirling designs along the river roadways.

Of predominant ailanthus:

>Clumps of hectic samaras
>caught in the giant webs
>of jungle fern-foliage.

I could be beginning the loaf I would serve you at dinner. In your absence, the preparation is the same. Flour, scalded milk, butter, boiling water, sugar, salt, yeast. Promised ball of dough.

Of the dandelion:

>Loss of perfect gold,
>perfect gain of grey,
>sphere-perfection dispersing perfectly.

My friends urge me to leave home for a while. They speak of *change*, of a holiday. They suggest I am becoming unduly attached to this apartment, these views, the astery edge of the river smouldering far below. I nod, and hover all the nearer the kitchen. Waiting for the dough to rise.

> Leavening of day,
> rise of light
> to fill the bowl of the world.

Staying home. Feeling relieved of my gadabout friends, who require to see for themselves the literal antipodes. Who Baedekerzealous enumerate every Zanzibar cat.

These hazy autumn mornings, I look the sun in its clean accessible coin of eye. Perimeter's clear. I scan circularity without being sun-struck.

How many bubbles in this rising dough? Reckless, I cut them away, cut in more flour.

Gull, mallard, pigeon rake instant black currents across the sun. But the plain medallion's known at a glance. Or was, until fires began to lick at the rim. Heat throbs in rings around the arising disk. I look, and look away. And everywhere small crazy blobs of sun flare brokenly in my blink of eyes. Morning goes up, vastly.

Friends gone, I'm left alone to observe our domestic sunrise inching east, these cooler mornings, landmark to landmark. That globe which set its ladder yesterday against a certain steeple, no longer mounts precisely there. Today it climbs against a longhaired chimney. A curious, congenial sensation in my body, of being more stable, more true-to-self, more authentic if stick-in-the-mud, than even our central star. I adhere.

Of bursting dandelion bubbles:

> Constant, the style is clinging
> to the firm achene:
> adrift in a feathery attendance.

I can't help praising a certain fixity. Remaining strictly in residence, I keep my faithful lookout. I can give eyewitness. The

OCTOBER

Harvest Moon that just hung over Cambridge, relies on me.
With something like personal reluctance at leaving, the lunar
glow has taken its own sweet long-lit time semicircling over me,
hour on gradual hour. Anyone who flew the Atlantic east last
night missed half the magic.

For Basho and Issa, travel was a pilgrimage. "Days and nights
are travelers of eternity." I have no desire to wander farther than
thought itself can take me—far enough indeed. To my stillstand-
ing threshold, the cloud-propelling wind brings pollen from dis-
tances. And takes my local, parochial seeds to the four corners.

> The terse milkweed pod
> still pursing its follicle tight.
> And somewhere a fastening loosens.

Of the butterfly weed:

> In season silently,
> out of the slender upstanding
> pods, the finely pubescent
> follicle minarets tapering
> greenly aloft in fall
> when turrets discolor to gaping
> verdigris:
>
> butterfly weeds
> of oval umber body
> winged with circular white
> floss, layer on layer
> leave their dehiscent muezzin
> porch for meccas of distant
> fields and roadsides where
> in time afire they rise
> and arrange air with an orange
> umbel,

> wearing such bright
> coronas of aureole summer
> they bear a numerous glory
> far into hallowed places
> from Maine to Minnesota,
> Florida to Mexico.

Moreover, I think my being here, still here, still usual, a provincial presence-in-the-flesh, confirms the pleasure of my friends' worldly circulation. There has to be someone at home to be shown those strenuous carvings purchased in person from far-flung natives, after eminent bargaining. That chipped mosaic secreted from an unguarded dig—the ravishing story's wasted on a fellow who's done it himself.

> Waste your wings on me!
> Such softness of feather exploding
> from milkweed dovecote.

Waste upon me the wide dust of your dispersion. All the more—now that you are released—I keep parochial attachment. You know where to find me.

The bonus of bread-making is the necessity to remain in close attendance. Dough acquires an imperative life of its own. It dictates when it must be tended: with more flour, firmer handling. While you lived, I made your bread, an emblematic lovemaking. To make bread now is a memorial act. It warms and exalts me all my homespun days. My friends bring home gifts of exotica. I invite them to break fresh bread.

By a sore stretch of analogy, I would have you return from journeying.

How unaccustomed your one-way going. Even astronauts plan on re-entry. The baking loaf you will not share, floats its aroma throughout the apartment. Neighbors sniff it in the corridor.

How poignant a penetration—a cutting edge.

> After the last mowing,
> the shore's no longer secret with tallness.
> Yet toppled aromas lift up the air.

Let me admit, my local excitements stun and stimulate me beyond all prospect of travel. I look down at a giant ash-tree cage, an amber sphere hung leaf-tremulous with garnets and carnelians. A maharajah might have commissioned the extravaganza to imprison divertingly his pet songbird. A freak five-minute snow, early and unofficial, blows through the bars almost horizontally: spray upon spray of—could be—migrating moths. Meanwhile a crimson champleve beetle crawls the longitudinous grand tour of my window, in search of outlandish winter accommodation. I'll look for him again come March.

In the pumpkin month of late October, cherry trees along the river turn pumpkin-color in a long curving line. How well they choose their season of change. *Something to think of when alone.*

As autumn surrounds and invades this modern highrise apartment, I begin to miss the hospitable presence of a fireplace. A hearth. Let the oven fill that lack. I make a shape of my need. I place my express longing in the care of electric heat. A chosen temperature browns my loaf.

> In the chill of October
> maples kindle their fire,
> a high open hearth.

While absent friends count lyrate gazelles ranging somewhere a protected veldt, I celebrate, beyond enumerating, the colors that come and go in the seas of treetops undulant beyond my window. Closer I praise the wild streaming week of herds of ladybugs roaming my terrace—in hundreds and hundreds. A box

*Isaac Watts

of gems of great price, they were bought for three dollars. They crossed the country from famous high-California hibernation, to rid my podocarpus of aphids. In my enchantment, I forget my original complaint, their original purpose. I feast my delight on this minim safari.

> Samara, capsule, berry
> follicle, acorn, pome—
> *long live the little!*

When I am most filled with the magnificence of these days of my life—suddenly I am most emptied of their meaning. The force that drains me is you. Piercingly I recall an ecstasy shared. Implausibly, I search for a way to draw you back into my continuing time, to remember you vividly into my future. Is it possible to persuade you into abidance?

> The mesh of wings that was this man:
> stretched, drawn out of shape, every sharing
> bird flown to its own chosen where.
> Nothing left at flock's core, no one.
> Then nothing's lost? Everything straightway gone
> on a purpose? a *now*? cleanly baring
> space of what was before, just before?
> The view's still changing. Take it, take it in,
> my slow eye! You're missing the breadth
> of flight and the fast terrible width
> of separations. Quick! See parts
> disperse, it seems, of one accord,
> his—can it be?—accord. Take
> hold of this, an opening, central truth.

O but what lovely things—I urge you—keep happening to those of us who stay put. Let us choose this place from which to watch the world. What need to explore otherworldly places? Departures are deprivals. You are foregoing, for the duration of your absence, this spouting, green-surging ailanthus. To think there was a time in historical time when no fountainous weed-trees soared from the ground of Massachusetts. Winter will soon unmask the solitary buds, the scars like shields commemorating defunct branches. I would not miss this favorite cold-weather sculpture for all the greenery in China. I would not have you miss this privileged outlook.

> From the green-and-gold bell-mouth
> of a wind-gonged ash-tree,
> leaves clang their hymning tongue.

How can I hear my single human discrepance while belfry-tumult engulfs me, my small pulse and refrain of person? If only the sounding would never stop.

While I have ears to listen, while I live, the sounding never stops. When the ash drops its oval clappers, the oak resonates all the more copperly. Boles hum, bare branches extend their legato phrases, till snow-accidentals tremble them. The measures of air fill up.

> Music comes to me where I am.

Come to me in music where I am. Things as they are, where they are: for such actualities journeys are joined. I stay and expect you, the ever-expanding variety of your immanence. Here, or nowhere, is where I meet you. Participate with me in my survival of you. Be the leaves of my tree.

The heart feeds on precise variety. And whether an ash leaf, emerging purplish, or maroon, or olive, sustains me less because I've already beheld a million turning leaves of the same tree define themselves—is, after all, a question of appetite. I taste the constant changes in the received *you*. I quicken to your manifest alterations.

A certain kind of want battens on intimacy. On what is pressed into the very wanting. Concentration of need. *Focus* is the Latin for hearth, or fireplace. I concentrate on baking my own good bread, the whole involvement from yeast through rising through kneading through rising and halving and rising and burnishing: and I savor hungrily the intricate differences from one miraculous loaf to another. I feed on the shapes of my want.

It is a last, a lasting supper:

> A half century later,
> I'm finally corning into the taste
> of separation. Really. That light piquant spread
> of distance we used to lay between us,
> was mere hunger-ration. This is a feast
> threatening never to end. Must I still eat?
>
> Must I, filled, still eat
> while the heavy banquet lasts later
> with every tolling month? To feast
> without relief is to lose the taste
> for food. Let there be small famines between us.
> Let such infinities as spread
>
> into malady, shrivel. Widespread,
> this table gluts me faint, for I eat
> the years. And still the board groans between us,
> heaping our division. Later, later!
> my tongue implores. Impossible to taste
> an undiminishing absence... But the feast
>
> insists. Famished for want of you, I must feast
> on want. Survival is my spread
> surfeit: grossly deadening, foretaste
> of death. O let me starve on live crumbs. To overeat

is morbidly to suffocate hunger. Later
I'll need that hunger—should there arise between us
some bare subsistence: some nothing between us,
an essence, in a place where feast
is a kind of fast. Later,

I think, eternity may spread
so sparse refreshment, we can eat
innocently again. Together we'll taste

the frugal air among our atoms: day-taste
and night-taste pure vintages between us.
Meal of simple starlight we can sheerly eat.
Dissolution itself shall serve our feast.
And should our particles be moved to spread
themselves galaxies apart, they'll plan later

reunions over the spread cloth of *later*.
We'll taste the aeons: between us—
a lovers' feast—break bread of extinction, eat.

LET: v. transitive, to permit, allow, suffer

Let November come in without knocking. For the year is a turning stile.

Let daybreak balance on chimneys. Morning's a circus, sun a star acrobat.

Let branches discount their leaf-losses, and compensate with buds. The stripped tree is the true tree. Let me learn its lineaments.

Let the pods hang poker-stiff, straight down from the catalpa bough. For they rule the inches of air. Winds can draw clean lines along them.

Cold is a consummate dyer. Let samaras bleach in the ailanthus cluster. Let them recall how once they blazed. Especially as winter overtakes me, let me draw the fires of your remembered presence about me. As memory wanes in the cold, I stoke all my urgency of reminiscence: summoning back what I need, reconstructing it.

Let fleece in the milkweed pod land its seed in a good soil. Let brave men imitate natural parachutists.

Let gutters remember the hectic leaf on the tree. For the luminous meteor is brought down as stone.

Let November prove capricious as March, so the housefly lingers outdoors in a May-like sun, and one bee still forages, one cricket chirps.

More than the sun, let rain glisten the pavement. How the month shines through its tears. Loss is a shower through which memory glows.

Let me whirl with the circuits of rainfall orbiting justly the pond-pewter river. Let me repeatedly perform a part I have not played before.

Let the gull arise from the river, leaving five circles behind her: her departure a skipped stone.

The fall of winter is an adze. Let the brilliant splinters of willow foliage be shaven down, to fleck the river with autumnal carp.

Let the lace-making wherry on the Charles weave faster than thread can last. Time itself directs the shuttle. And time disperses the pattern. Penelope is time's daughter. Let me study her making and her unmaking.

Let world, my great oak-apple gall, compass me round with mottled symmetry. I am the larva that feeds among the fibers.

Let Jupiter, that glabrous spider, dominate the dusk, a diamond punctuation in our sentence of early gloom.

Let Venus, unseen lovelight, tinder-seed, drift its fiery thistledown into my cold dark. Let my bed take deep the imagined tuft of ember-grain, my soil stoke up sparks.

Let the meniscus moon hone its dagger against the sharpening dusk.

Let my longing range a diaspora without let. The worst thing for a woman is to feel at home.

Let yellow witch hazel deliver its final touseled strategy, and last year's seeds beat a four-note tattooing retreat from the pod. How far our children explode from the parent bush! Let them break our branch, and use it to find wellsprings. Let them use us as a demulcent when they are sore.

Let the orange berries of bittersweet come out of pale husks into their own brilliance. The vine's flowering was lost among louder demonstrations. Now it vies with the crimson sumac shout. Let loss find an orange berry in the broken husk, keep opening its pale breast to the passerby month. The wild rose haw itself holds less of brilliance.

Let the larch persist as a last torch in the draining light.

Let asters linger as long as they dare. This is the month of last things.

Let a few honeybees still loiter outside the hive. Their work is done. They merely stretch their muscles.

Let early snow lie like a foam on the shores of the river, and magic the water to molten tar. Let a day-moon be a blob of un-fallen surf overhead. Let me be the constant beholder.

O let the moon at mid-month set early, that there be black dark-ness in which the Leonids may fall, gems in a scattering neck-lace. Let me be watching when a drop of mercury delineates a star. And you, o deepest memory, you be my midnight. From wells of shade, feed my secret spark: this luminous beetle, this lesser star. If you were day, your light would drain my smaller sun. Be dark for me: a dark sea wresting from arid noon the leap of the pearl-diver. Be my deep disclosure.

Let a fierce northwest wind rev up the leaves, and scatter them from their starting-place. Let the starting-speed be but great enough, a body will escape completely from earth. Must you run south before the wind?

Let a soft warm westerly breeze apologize, so infant spiders may hatch, and climb, and launch their kite-tails adrift across baring branches. Twigs shimmer in the gossamer light. Let every new-born thought of you sparkle in the afternoon sun. There will be long nights of winter. There will be hibernaculum fissures and crannies. I stay and watch the things that move.

Let the countryman tell me of foxes basking lazily in the late November glow. Let their coats be orange color of fire. Let them yawn disdainfully as I dream I pass them.

Let the blackbird flash a last red-winged salute. Chickadees and juncos, jays and tree sparrows keep me cold company. Praise over-winterers.

Now let the mushroom moon rise in a dark meadow: uplifted chanterelle. Who raised it, the goblet? A health to what waste heath or rotted log?

Let ghosts of summer veil all familiar autumn traits. Even strangeness is company.

Let me rake the river with my eyes. A certain hunger needs to be kept going to sea. Some wants are swifter than water can slake. I parch. The tines loosen longingly.

And over and over let daybreak jimmy apart this house. Let me seize again the morning I thought so steadily to own. Every tak-ing leaf of me cants east.

Let the willow streamers still uphold the air goldenly, a firm yellow froth. Let me lean the weight of my eye on their accom-modating crests.

Alders, be fixed of resolve, frozen purple with catkin endurance. No matter that March will stretch the two, then three, four mus-cular inches. No matter they'll go soft, go gold.

Let fungus scallop the crumbling log. Frills and ruches disguise an aging throat.

Let fire in the west consume only the husk of tomorrow, not the core.

Let fog unfurl its cloth: a magician's bag. More metaphor than scene, figure than fact, a sane delusion. What veils you from me could be less than I believe.

Let memories lie like shadows flat on the street, angled to their tree or post. They may look lifeless, two-dimensioned replicas, dull, dark, compared to the original uprights on the tree-lawn: not steadfast, not real. But watch the way those shadows refuse to be run over! They rise up and waylay cars, buses, ambulances—throwing their non-weight around whatever body runs between them and the root of their being. They embrace hood, chassis, trunk, with a great crooked clasp. They press their sign on the least intercepting child. When he's gone, they lie down.

Let metaphor help me lift your loss on board. The burden lies above sea level, a ready anchor. Too heavy to raise by hand, it's wound by marvelous image of rope and drum. It moves with me anywhere I sail. It frees me to move. For I am the windlasser.

DECEMBER

But. But is a place where they can cease to distress her
                                        —Gertrude Stein

The last home fires went out for us eight years ago, when we
moved to the fifteenth floor of a new high-rise apartment build-
ing. We left behind us four fireplaces and the upkeep of a large
and aging house.

How to live without a hearth?

I have spoken of baking bread.

Now I turn to the sun—whether clouded or revealed—more often,
more searchingly. And in the night hours I wait for the break
of day with livelier expectancy. I can't kindle a true hearth-fire
in the meantime. Can't turn inward in the apartment toward a
prim makeshift sun-symbol. I abide only half *at home*; the other
half turns *away*. A kind of indoor-outdoor survival.

The fireplaces I knew—in those hearthside days—were all situated
against inner walls. So I turned my back on windows, to watch
a homemade altar flicker and flame. To think of the times I've
neglected the piercing look of outdoor things, in favor of the
dreamy warmth, the domesticity of blazing logs. Wood is our
only self-renewing fuel, I've told myself mystically.

Prometheus served us too well. His theft has tamed us. We're
so taken with this technic of ignition, we're drawn away from
exploring those universal fires: the light of day and of dusk, the
stars in *their* flame and flicker. How often, I wonder, would I
walk out onto my balcony, these fierce winter nights, if I lay

snug in the reach of a hearth, lulled to ease in the conviction that the focal point, the sacred place of this household was the fire I'd built and kindled? To think I might have missed those mid-December Geminids, each star a celestial drop of mercury sliding down a chute of sky!

Defenders of the hearth speak of 'primal need', and 'sanctuary'. That prim radiance at the foot of the chimney is a most modest reminder of our prime flagrant source. The great sun that saves our planet from extinction is daintily idealized across the andirons. A lenient compromise takes the token for the burning immensity. The hearth is comforting, of a comfortable human size. The metonymy allays our major homage. The small sign 'makes do' for the enormous thing signified.

No great harm, granted, in enjoying the home fires. No great hazard, either. No risk of encountering that huge burning presence which confronts us under the skies. If, in these northern latitudes, we turn indoors in winter, at least we can turn back to the windows through which that presence shines or dims or darkens. Most days and nights, I'm glad my windows reach from ceiling to floor, drafts and all. I rejoice in this fifteenth storey site, the strenuous exposure, the unmitigated two hundred and eighty-five degrees of view. I do regret a little fire on firedogs—but not often, not vastly.

> Who has laid that fire
> which catches at an eastern tinder?
> Myself, by watching?

What a bold spirit I make of myself!

For a rash moment I forget that it was you who stood between me and the raging light of day: a protection, a distancing, lightyears of conduit, reducing the awful hazard of that fire. To live in your ambience was to be warmed and flushed benignly, by your heat and hue. Direct rays of life which, unmediated, convey death as well as growth, came channeled through you, came gentled.

The sun itself proved its best energy through you: its destructive power converted, transformed by your space of mediation.

In this time of absence, I look again to the depot sun to supply me through your far-reaching influence. For I have discovered you still permeate the distances of space. Though I need the stark basic light of day, though I require the means of growth, I continue to receive them through a life-maintaining memory. You mitigate that first fire-force into a tenderness which keeps my plants, my purposes greening.

Eight months of your absence, and still you speed billions of miles to my side. In a sense more sun than ever—liberated as you are from earthling data—nonetheless you maintain a controlling, ameliorating presence. We once called it love.

I still call it love, remembered love. By virtue of that relationship—which can bind the most disparate phenomena—I accept my life in the world. I enjoy a tolerable fire, I receive a bearable light. I partake of you in the world: in the white gull over the river and the black one below; in the pyracanthus keeping its green leaves and orange-headed pomes; in the Cold Moon that arcs over my head all night and wakes me by morning. What would otherwise destroy me and the things of my world, you bring acceptably, gladly, to my door.

Everywhere in my life I learn to know your conduit energy. You teach me—more than ever was possible while you had a name and a distinct location—to know you in natural recurrences of time and space: trees, grass, flowers, their lift and fall. You live in the pronoun you. It encompasses even your loss. So long as the rhythm of nature persists, you prevail. There is no desolation, no ultimate loneliness. You are present.

Presence is only a matter of close attention. Then earlier distractions and preoccupations dissipate. I become all one intense perception. Like Confucius, so delighted by the sound of a carillon, he forgot for three months on end to notice what he was eating.

Like air, let me live
in the sound of your music.
Be the carillon of my city.

Let me change the name of death to *music*, as Jews once changed the name of a very sick man, to obviate the final event.

That year in Ghent, we lived in the sound of the belfry: the very cobbles resonated, the tuberose begonias in the walled garden. Splinters of glass topped the wall, to keep out neighboring cats. Unhindered, music poured down over us. Damp air held the music like drops of moisture. The mist-music trembled the splinters, drenched our pulses. Every winding canal, a tapetum, lifted upward, vividly, the clanging utterances: as rays of light in the eyes of nocturnal animals are reflected back from a crystalline layer, thus increasing vision in the dim illumination. O I was aware enough, wit-warm enough in life, to value your mortal splendor, the metal of your instrument. Yet death is the bruising stroke.

Death is the beat of clapper on bell,
releasing a bound essential music.
And I am listening.

Listening, I am all suspense. I am waiting, in that watchful tension where everything is happening, everything is surprising, possible, new. As once in Flanders, where everything was strange, where for a year we attended, alert and seeking, to signs and intimations, hoping to define the essential Flanders. Carillon? cobbles? canal? pollarded willow? But these things themselves are but diffuse signals. The self, the self!

Your self, how I keep hoping to define it.

Let me begin more modestly. With the pollarded willow. With a tree, any tree. A tree self. Where to find it?

In the deep golden heartwood, surely: center, support, the bole's beginning? Core of the past that lives, as ancestry survives in all our longing, reaching, branching. That gives us pith.

Or likely in the white sapwood cells, those annual widening hoops, conduits of water, of minerals, fluids and foods, upwards and crosswise. And always open-ended to let need through.

What of the blanket cambium, slender protector from tip to root, increasing, dividing, functional, feverish, torn between turning to sapwood inwards, and outwards to phloem? Might be in changeful phloem some steadfast essence?

Tubes that bear down, and down, a juice from wealthy foliage, green nurture to the base? Elongate ducts that sieve, send, appease earthbound necessity. That keep the column strong upon the plinth. And make an arbor move.

Veritably in the stretching bark—that cracks to cork and death, like waves that break and perish—the tree's held true, the sea's held bound. A surface miracle no less contains me in my desquamating skin.

And round that bark a spiral girds the parts. Limbs, leaves and buds are winding, lawfully ascending, like strings round tops, like snail chambers. In principle, a spiral drives the bole to reach the summit. A spiral draws the tree to be.

Words. Analogies. I ponder. I posit. But quintessence eludes me. And yet. Though I cannot define, though I cannot name, not essentially, yet I can speak of *you*, and know, somehow, what that pronoun signifies. I can discover approximations. Through the intervention of images I can touch you. And through this conjunction you can reach me, even intercede for my life. Through this obdurate transaction. This insistent *nevertheless*.

Now let me cup my hands and hold the sun
between my palms as though it were your face
I kept. The touch is warm. The shape agrees
with plane and curve I knew. I think the bone
within the round of air. I think the man,
the flesh. I think I feel the past, and press
too hard. I break the cup I made. I lose
the light it bound. The light lies spilled upon
the earth. I stand in it. I let it lie
around me large as I would have your love
take place. You fill the wind. I breathe your breath.
You keep me, and I call my life the day.
You deepen, and I live the night. I live
in time a bowl you cup my being with.

So here it is at last, the distinguished thing
—Henry James

O to live forever in transience, in the serene amazement of pro-
gress toward an inaccessible destination. Like lying suspended
in mid-air on my high balcony—in this January thaw—between
two luminous bodies: the light I can't directly confront over-
head, and the perceived token-sun in the river below. Always
between, between...

On this torpid Cambridge morning, three ovals incubate under
the far-off doll-size Larz Anderson Bridge.

> Diorama views of watery upside-down faerie—
> streamlet, paper-thin shore-edge,
> tree-top, head-stand chimney—
> invite the eye of childhood
> long since shuttered.

The air's candied with unseasonal dazzle. I'm lifted off my deck-
chair, a kind of levitation, where facts, assignments, achieve-
ments—both what have been and what are to be—transcend their
limited designations. Where it's logic enough, indeed wholly
and suspensefully fulfilling, to exist in this very condition which
is no-place, being sheer possibility, pure unregulated availabil-
ity. With no concern about duration—of light, of location, of
this transit equilibrium. Without interest in starting points or
finish lines. Liberated, for a perfect nonce, from afterwards
and before, from there and there. Open, here, welcoming the
prodigal spending of day. Receptive, taking endless pattern-

ings of sun-sparks which constantly alter the slate-gray stream: into facsimiles of diamond-studded fish, hugely jeweled water spiders, river-borne giant dragonflies, now clear-winged, now glinting grumose. The delusive wherry-wakes never quite completed—that is, their completions never determinable. For all one can guess, the foam has sunk into the depths and continues its streaming and revising profoundly under the surface and out to sea. The circles left by oar-strokes never quiet, never quite definable. The prowing mallards embarked in topaz-fire.

Never to be on the verge of saying: Now, in this split instant the unending *present* must come to a halt. An ecstasy of presence. And while it lasts, no need to question: is it desirable? perishable? repeatable?

To construe each moment into unceasing transition, where root, rock, rower—all are loosened from whatever rigor might have established them in a vanished time. Where objects are not reaching the fixed delineations toward which they seem always to be tending. To sustain this clearing in the thicket of experience, where longing—a lance—is forever soaring, soaring, never arriving, nor falling. For its metal has no measure, no gravity, but gleams all process, a hurling, an Excalibur forged in a smithy superior even to renowned Gassan's, who, Basho tells us, must have chosen to temper his swords in a certain crystal-clear stream near Mount Yudono, because of a mysterious power in the water.

The weightless shaft of the imagination, the smoky evanescence and incandescence of wind-swept flurries on the river, licking, larruping, darting, developing, torsading too swiftly for keeping. And too swiftly, I gladly concur, for losing. Even the polluting chemicals become suddenly other: enormous burrowings of brownish-saffron eels under the river's skin. And the skin-current itself a series of cloudridges, horizons, Milky Ways, lunulas...

To abide, to inhere in such transience, without reservation, volitionally, urgently. In the certainty that within this performance, this flow of surgings and resurgings, coalescences and dispersions, in this momentous avowal and perspective, lies time's true management.

Not to fear dissolution: yours, or mine, or the world's. To take pleasure in dissolution, as one enjoys beholding the dissolving shapes of clouds. To see one's self, one's life, one's beloved, as a cloud, endlessly changing contour, endlessly forming and dissipating. To live in the watching of one's life. Without interruptions for the world's work, or demands, or definitions. In the awareness of dissolution, to become one with the process of dissolution. Never denying, never resisting it. To dissolve, finally, the antagonism between being and becoming. As love dissolves the duality of lovers. Longing and fulfillment identical—because ecstasy has merged their outlines in a momentous embrace.

To ignore significances—because significance isolates facts, determining their status in the universe. As if that were desirable. No, facts are fleeting. Let them go. They're all too alike, as dust-motes, interchangeable. As statistics. As natural phenomena. As mankind.

Let go, let go details. Yield to the great uniform solitude. A marvelous universal stupor of will, where golden mornings and mauve dusks are equally welcome because distinctions have been cancelled in the grip of a terrible destroying fist. Creative because destroying. To live creatively, in the creative surge. To exist solely as process, never requiring to detain the shape of an instant into some longer form. To be willing, glad, to die each instant because that death is the very birth of the next instant. To destroy identity, yours as well as mine, in the ardor of a living death. In favor of an all-embracing uniformity, ultimate guarantee against separation.

> Insisting on sticks, stones, sponges,
> oats, ossuaries, oranges,
> is to overlook nameless water, how it interchanges

itself freely. If I can remember
to call you ocean: waves without number
comprising every angle and camber

of tide, if I can widen
your name to hold hidden
rivers, minerals, mermaiden

lagoons bluer than longing,
steam and ice and the singing
talk of whales, the salt tonguing

of foam, stretch and fusion
of dew...If I explode my notion
of singular recall into sea-fission

so particled even the old atom
sunders, the cherished item
bursts: all freedom, freedom.

o then absence is nothing
less than presence: a breathing
out, in, out, life, death.

To drop the pen from the fingers, loosen resistance from the grasp of thought. To yield up this last defense against anonymity. Because only the anonymous is lasting. In the name of love, to surrender all other names. Let our love be anonymous. So consuming is the need that love be lasting.

Not choose not to be
—Gerard Manley Hopkins

Without you, today, the sun rises at 6.49 a.m., sets at 5.11 p.m.

Without you, the length of the day is 10.22.

Without you, the moon rises at 6.37 a.m., sets at 6.02 p.m.

Without you, the day of the year is 42.

Without you, headlights should be turned on at 5.16 p.m.

Without you, the moon is New today at 12.17 a.m.

Without you, the moon's phases are as follows:

> First Quarter, Feb. 20, 2.39 a.m.
>
> Full Moon, Feb. 25, 9.15 p.m.
>
> Last Quarter, Mar. 4, 4.20 p.m.

Without you, the mean Boston temperature yesterday was 17 degrees. This was a departure from normal of -13 degrees.

Without you, the Departure this month was -43 degrees, the Departure this year plus 151 degrees.

Without you, the total precipitation this month to date is 1.31 inches.

Without you, there is a chance of occasional light snow today. High temperatures in the low 30s, winds becoming southeast 10 to 15 mph.

Without you, it is still important to have a TRAVEL FORECAST:

Albany	Snow	17/31
Anchorage	Clear	08/05
Atlanta	Clrng	46/66, etc. etc.

Without you, tonight, there will be occasional light snow ending, low temperatures in the upper 20s.

Without you, tomorrow, cloudy, chance of occasional light snow or rain. High temperatures in the mid to upper 30s.

Without you, NOW, free checking with 5% interest at the Boston Five.

Without you, I may learn to DEVELOP CONFIDENCE, Speak Effectively, Attend a Free Explanation Meeting of the DALE CARNEGIE COURSE.

Without you, I may bring this coupon for a Free Shrimp Appetizer and a Baked Potato with Our Prime Rib Dinner at Emerson's Ltd.

Without you—but I am over 60—I might have trained, day or evening, to be a professional bartender under simulated cocktail lounge conditions.

Without you—on the next page—I may read my LEO horoscope: *Follow hunches now to gain your objectives. An idea or two from your mate can also be of help.*

Without you, I can skip the crossword puzzle, as always.

Without you, a mockingbird perches on my fifteenth storey railing—striking my dullest month to a moment's dazzle quicker than *Thanks, mime!*

Without you, at dawn, Mars can be found in the sky, in Sagittarius, in the southeast, until daylight hides it. Are you a star that shines only by day? Is it the light of day that obscures your presence? What kind of identification do I demand?

That time you jumped into your jitney and raced up to see me in Maine. I'd hurt my back an over-arching swan dive! and you wanted to examine me yourself. Stopped en route for speeding, you had no driver's license, no papers of any kind on your person. You had come directly from the laboratory, in your 'hospital whites'. You were you, all right, no 'unnecessary duplicate' . How *you* you were—no one more so. A shining identity. But the police required a sign, a thread of evidence. Something *not* you—to prove you. There you were, wholly, perfectly yourself. But not demonstrably so. Not in the eyes of the Maine lawman. The irony of the situation caught you. I can see the laughter glinting your eyes. You undid the buttons of your fly, and opened your trousers. Stitched at the waist, in red, your name, and the name of the hospital. Saved by a laundry-mark!

Am I, humorless law-woman, demanding some laundry-mark or other?

Without your laundry-mark, snow falls, meteors radiate, shadowbands ripple. Shadowbands that are present at all times but are visible only during an eclipse. Because of their low light, they can hardly be seen against a sunlighted ground. They move too swiftly to be caught in an unblurred picture. Yet perhaps just before and just after totality of a solar eclipse...

Without you, regardless of you, the moon is at apogee. Do you orbit elliptically about me? Are there times of month when you are 'farthest' from me?

Without you, day after tomorrow, I shall look sharply into the evening twilight and see the slender crescent moon. A little later, as the sky darkens, Venus and Jupiter, two bright objects, will appear below and to the right of the moon, much closer to the horizon: Venus to the right and the brighter of the two. The precise predictability of the stars underscores the vagueness of your whereabouts.

How good it is to welcome Venus again as a clear evening star. Last winter seems only last month. The reliability of the planets moves me to a suffusing gratitude. To detect a recurrence in the midst of weltering transitions is to satisfy an inmost need. Fulfillment of such need calls for praise. The occurrence is a great melody that surprises every time I hear it—even though I know it by heart. The small variants of juxtaposition that happen from year to year, cannot change the basic movement. They simply improvise tenderly around it. "Improvisation," says Ruby Braff, "is adoration of the melody." I listen to keep hearing your melody.

Without you, the melody of the skies continues.

Now Venus and Jupiter will move closer. By the 17th they will be at their closest, less than a lunar diameter apart. Seldom, says the Sky Chart, will you see two such bright planets so close together. They almost seem to touch in the sky. Hereafter they will separate. But they will meet again. I cling to the image of their recurrence.

A perturbation, a rippling, sporadic presence, a scintillation...a turbulence, an agitation of airs of differing densities...a twinkling such as we attribute to stars separated from us by turbulent distances. The world continues to be. Without you, if I insist, your laundry-mark. But *with* you, *with* you! Because you could not choose not to be. Because transitions alter nothing essentially. Despite baffling changes. Not once in all the millions of times I have looked down at the river, has it looked the same as at one other time. Yet I sing *The Charles, The Charles!*

For everything is double. It is what it is, and what it is becoming. And therefore we should be taking a liberty in denying it—however alien or absent it might seem in transition. For it becomes only itself, over and over and over. This is its only way to be. And if I miss your face as I remember it—that is because the heart has a slothful beat, and accepts most readily what is steadfast and familiar.

Teach my pulse to quicken truthfully. Seat me 'sultanically among the moons of Saturn', let me see you as you are, a wonder and a grandeur. Let the world continue happening, from daybreak to new daybreak. And *with* you, surely, somehow, always.

What thou lovest well, shall not be reft from thee
—Ezra Pound

Month of promise, month of clues. Deprivations of winter are mostly past. Now I may look for inklings: earlier light, yellowing willow-whip, gold flash of coltsfoot.

A first ladybug!

> Someone must have wound her up.
> By the time I see the lacquer-red match-tip hemisphere,
> animated as a toy beetle,
> she's halfway up inside my window.
> Panting, her machinery rises into almost-spring.
> My eyes climb on her pupil-black spots.
>
> O the splendid animation of her six hair-breadth legs.
> It ticks her like clockwork toward the sun.
> It unsprings her to get her flat black belly
> slid onto the first fortunate leaf.
> Then short shrift to aphids!

Month of promise, month of search. Search following loss. For without loss, there is no search, no *living in search*, the greatest adventure. Before the occurrence of loss, there is only the possibility of loss. True, this contingency gives poignance, a certain pang, to each hour of possession. The question, *How long?* hovers over the fullest bliss, crow-shadow flitting between lovers and the sun. But the shadow is momentary, and due, indeed, to the splendid presence of light.

Lovers' bliss, like the world itself, is an unearned happiness, a gift of the sun. And while it lasts, right-spirited lovers enjoy it. Why should they question it? Praise it, yes. And give thanks for it. A gold coin in the hand. A gold accident. A discovery, in a way. We happened, suddenly, upon each other. Though we had not even known, distinctly, we were searching. Something fortuitous about the incident. We were more "casting about" than searching. Wondering, half-heartedly, if there was something to search for. When suddenly it was bestowed.

We could afford to be wastrel. We had not paid for our luck.

Now is the time of reckoning. I search the past, to give it its due. The way is exact, a return over known terrain. Now that I have lost you, the search has become serious, specific. As I go forward into the past, I retrace the history of love to where its origin is experienced a further time. Such earnest re-tracking would never have occurred to me while we moved together. While your foot touched earth beside mine, I rarely glanced down to watch your footprint.

Now is the moment of reversal. I go back over this trail to establish a new find, a true find, evidence that there was this journey taken together, and before the journey there was the meeting. I search for what cannot be taken from me: that this love happened.

I thirst to discover the past. I parch for the wine of the past.

> Sometimes it curls and climbs
> the unsuspecting side of a crystal goblet
> I start to take in hand.
>
> Even before I raise it,
> meaning to tip the container to my mouth,
> the vessel bleeds grape-dark

toward the rim, toward me,
up unguessed arteries. The draught's lifting
with a slow will of its own,

even the dregs declining
to lie low now. I watch and slake thirst
strangely merely beholding

wine without consuming.
Soon I will parch only for the grace of vision.
I will stay, if I can,

in the one-sixth gravity
of the moon, and see fire rising to eye level,
undowned, unquenched...

There is a way into the past. I go back over it.

What new discoveries are possible in reversal! Every inch of ground teems with life. Ground we covered swiftly, lightly, with little need for pause. Now I go slowly back, examining the imprints: where we walked in unison, where we fell apart, where you strode on ahead, where you waited for me to catch up. And under our prints the ground seethes with its own being: soil and stone, seed and spore, slug, snail, larva, mite, rotifer.

And if I should now discover that as I walk the earth, walk the globe, I am walking its circumference? Round and round and round? O then surely, repeatedly, I'd come upon the place from which I had started this search. I'd be back here, again, after circumambulation. But richer each time, bearing fresh knowledge of past journeys, bringing experience around to this very moment, over layers of history. Time as a sphere. Is it not worth considering? Is it not a more persuasive metaphor than the endlessness of a line? Our imagination demands conformance to what we can grasp. We hold a ball in hand, even toss it up and catch it again. But—*infinity*? Can we take hold of the idea? Really *live* it?

Loss as an infinite phenomenon. Can I really know what I mean? How could I even entertain the conception—finite item that I am? Sheer wordplay. And then to think I might dare, somehow, to *reverse* the speculated process: back from infinity! No, it's far too desperate an effort. Too violent a pairing of the specific and the unbounded. Love requires a tenderer notion.

I propose loss as a circling—an unnumbered circling, if you will, a round-the-universe journey, during which the past is repeatedly come upon. Love, and the lover, thus recoverable. I propose, in the absence of evidence to the contrary, that time moves so as to come back upon itself. The lost lover moves in time, coming back upon the hours of love, the beloved. We are making the same journey, you and I, this circumambience of ours. Sooner or later—if you dawdle, or I hurry—one of us again overtakes or intersects the other. We go the same ways, backwards or forwards, no matter. For we follow the sphere. We travel the great circles of the sphere, and are never farther from each other than the universal antipodes. And often closer, even abreast.

> Now from the other side of time,
> speak to me as the whale
> sings across that curvature
> of water which confines sound
> so it carries halfway round
> the churning world. Let our wide
> abyss become a room.
> You need not raise your voice
> against a loud universe:
> no other wave-length curves
> through distance like your word.
> I listen for your undertone.

This spherical shape of time bodes well for the future. Separation is no infinitely stretched-out course, measured in days, months, anniversaries. It brings us round again, exactly, to a meeting-point, to just where we were: for the thousandth time.

Or the trillionth. Time itself is the one sphere. Only the numbers of times we circle it are numberless.

Hence—o blessed hence—we—you—have never *left*. For it is well known that he who returns never went away—*away* being that direction we indicate with a tangent, the destination of which suggests infinity, terrible unreturning infinity.

I propose, then, yes, that we were always on course, on this circular course. Look! the month is making its spring arc! Every point en route is a turning-point as well as a record. Once again the elm, that Miocene reminder, comes curving into the year's March, one circuit more, one more loosening of brown bud-scales in a coppery mist. Alders, willows, poplars, maples so predictable in their early start. They move to the cycling of time as to a roundelay. Catkins unseal the gum that binds them. Their mouths open, and sing.

Memory was the culprit. It forgot those prior, even prehistoric journeys, those flowerings before what we called a first day, a first meeting—journeys over the identical world-track, but minus our names, as we moved in the same rounds. Now that I know, now that I have remembered, I have to tell this quiet gospel.

> Mid-March, and the sycamore
> still celebrates, ornamented
> as Christmas, but tarnished
> the tawny bells reminiscing
> their tidings.
> That's
> how I'd like to sing,
> soft as a plush burr
> jarring no lightweight spell
> of mid-morning, just minding
> the fragile air, humming
> the whole good news.

Circulation is our history, our bloodstream, the wholeness of our lives. It is all we know. And how much it is! The recovering over and over and over again of our past. Through the act of our present, our future. Nothing lost, nothing for long left behind. Left, but only to be returned to. Altered, in the sense of *added to*. Recovered.

> Recover me, recover
> our time
> over and over and over.
> Let the imperative rhyme
> with the lover.

Poet, concert singer, actress, novelist, translator; wife, mother, grandmother, widow.

Norma Holzman Farber (1909-1984) was the author of more than thirty books. Her poems appeared in periodicals including *The New Yorker*, *The Nation*, *The Christian Science Monitor*, and *The New York Times*; artists illustrating her books included Petra Mathers, Arnold Lobel, Trina Schart Hyman, and Tomie dePaola; composers including Daniel Pinkham set her words to music.

At eighteen, in 1927, Norma Holzman married Sidney Farber, pioneer in the chemotherapy of cancer, legendary for his care of the ill. He died in 1973.